I Make My Bed I Lie In It

JANET TAI

INDIA • SINGAPORE • MALAYSIA

CONTENTS

INTRODUCTION

I am a Malaysian Chinese aged 64 years old. I am a breast cancer and a marital abuse survivor. This book of confessional poetry is a culmination of my forty plus years in a bad marriage. The title of this book **I MADE MY BED I LIE IN IT** is an English idiom which explains that we must accept the consequences of our actions and choices even if they are unpleasant.

I thought I had made the right choice in marrying a man who is eleven years my senior. I married for love and commitment but apparently my spouse had other ideas. Throughout our married years many issues cropped up and I began to see him for who he is. There were issues with his siblings, conjugal neglect, conjugal abuse which led cancer to come for me. I survived cancer and I thought I was free from the abuse but far from that. It only stopped for good when he suffered a mild stroke.

This book also includes the story of my unhappy childhood which played a part in my miscalculated judgement of my choices. I was never loved as a child as I was adopted. To be fair life went south only after nine years old when my foster mom passed away. My biological father gave me up because he was gender bias as I was the third daughter in a row. After I left, he fathered six boys. My only blessing that came from being adopted was that I had a much better education.

It is now at this plateau of peace that I am putting this book out. My love for poetry stemmed from college days as an English Literature student. This book is an effort that took three years of writing. Inspiration comes from my soul as we are deeply connected. I write almost every day. Sometimes it could be about my childhood or my bad marriage. I talked a lot about loneliness and finally learning to heal. I also talked about the hope of finding love and the feeling of being in love again.

Slowly with the help of my therapist I am on the mend and I do put out a couple of cheerful poems. This book is also for those women going through the same predicament as I and I hope that it will encourage and inspire them to know that they are not alone.

HOPE SPRINGS ETERNAL

Janet Tai

18/04/2025

THIS BOOK IS DEDICATED TO

Mr. RALPH DILLION HACKETT - my sponsor

JACQUELINE NG YEE LING – my bestie who always stepped up to help me pronto

LAU YOKE FHAN – my sister in Christ who is an absolute epitome of kindness

To all my virtual fellow poets/poetess and friends who knows me and constantly serve as my supporters. You know who you are.

I DID NOT SIGN UP FOR THIS

When I affirmed my marriage vows
I thought you did too
I thought you would appreciate
How hard I fought for you

Oh! Woe is me
I was young
Foolish and naïve
You! You with your
Honeyed tongued words
The charmer

You got your trophy wife
While all the time
I was committed to
Building us a home
Your wily ways came undone

That was as far as I

Allowed my nostalgia

To travel

I can't bear to remember

I grabbed my head

When the PTSD surfaced

Those spasms gripped me

As I lay in the foetal position

Until those spasms calmed down

I berated myself for not

Listening to my elders

Forty plus years

Forty freaking plus years

I gave you my youth and my life

I believed in you to prove

My family wrong

Now as I lie in yoga's

DEAD MAN'S POSE

Staring at the ceiling thinking

I've been waiting for my freedom
Twenty plus years had passed
I shouted out loud
GOD! WHEN IS MY TIME!!!

REBEL FOR A LOST CAUSE

I am a woman of 64
Married young at 21
Had my first child at 22
I know! I know!
You must all think
I'm bonkers

At that coming of age
Fresh young 'crispy'
Virgin
Life was a start of
Endless possibilities
To be discovered

Hold your horses
Let me explain
Growing up in a
Authoritarian family
My life was pretty
Much mapped out

Get into the university
Graduate with a degree
Marry another graduate
Hopefully those in the
Career line of a
Banker/accountant/lawyer

So, you see
My life is not mine to own
Thus, a rebel I became
Just to dislodge myself
From my family's stronghold
My choice, my bad

What I thought was a
Man of honor
Turned out to be the
Opposite
Thus began my
Forty plus years of nightmare

Each time he crossed
The boundary of character
I would put an imaginary pin to it
It had accumulated to so many

That I had lost count
I resigned in regret

It's been forty plus years
I gave myself to this family
No one can fault me for not
Doing my job
I bore the brunt of every
Adversity

At this juncture of my life
I have discharged my duties
With flying colors
My sons became
Good prospects for
Future wives

Their father
The man in the next room
Have nothing in common with me
The day he abused me
Puts an end to everything
He is as good as dead to me

I started this family as a
Rebel with a cause
The man in the next room
My supposedly 'better half'
Had relegated me to a foolish
Rebel for a lost cause

SEPTEMBER'S TRIGGERS

18.09.1982 – I got married

18.09.2003 – I was diagnosed with cancer

18.09. 2009 – I had a hysterectomy

This is no fluke

It was really meant to be

If it happened once

One might call it

A coincidence but

On the third time

It is really fate

Oh! September 18

How you wreak havoc

Into my life

With all those

Heartbreaking encounters

You took away

Parts of me

That defines my femininity
It took me twenty plus years
To come to terms with it

Once again, I'm made to
Relive those
Dark memories
With your incoming
Presence

Well! I've got news for you
You can no longer taunt me
Those memories
Don't bother me anymore
I will not cry pity

The past cannot be undone
I've got caring virtual
Friends
Who's got my back
You!!! Can go fly kite

SEPTEMBER 18TH

September of 1982
The 18th. morning
I left my maiden home
A married woman
I thought I had wedded
Into the arms of
A forever love
Instead, it was
Out of the frying pan
Straight into the fire

September of 2003
The 18th. morning
Sitting at the surgeon's
Clinic
Thumbs playing
Twiddle dee twiddle dum
Anxiously awaiting
The medical outcome

I am sorry, said the surgeon
It is CANCER
With a grim look on his face

September of 2009
The 18ᵗʰ. morning
Clad in a surgical gown
A hysterectomy scheduled
Waiting anxiously
In my wheelchair
Outside the operating theatre

September morning
You and I
We go way back
We have come a long way and
You're the epitome of
All that is bad in my life

PIECES OF ME

1982
A very significant
Year
The year 1 obtained
My 'MRS' degree

I was tutored and came
From the
School of Hard Knocks
I thought 1 had
Graduated well

Sadly
It was not so
Apparently
I had more
Learning to do

In that process
I had started

Developing 'cracks'
That would
Gradually break me

1983 to 2018
I had been broken
Into a heap of
Complete mess
Just like Humpty Dumpty

As time moves on
Painstakingly 1
Picked up the broken pieces
To tediously put them back
Together again

All those cracks
All those brokeness
Almost took me
To the point of
No return

Without
Professional help
Without self- love

Healing is
Impossible

I am on the mend
Bits and pieces of
My brokeness
Are slowly
Being restored

However, all those scars
In my heart that overlapped
Will never ever be
Smoothen out again
It has now morphed into PTSD

———————————————

SELF IMPOSED CELIBACY

I was in my mid thirties
When my spouse came up
To me one day to inform me
That he has decided to go into
Self-imposed celibacy

I was stunned because
It wasn't a discussion but
Merely a conveying of information
His reason was he's too stressed
Just like that he left me high and dry

Since that was his call
I focused all my attention
Into raising my boys wholeheartedly
The question of conjugal neglect was
Left at the back burner

Time dragged on
It was one of the most miserable

Period of my life – as a wife has
Needs that a selfish spouse
Does not take into consideration

That was my life for five long years
My heart had frozen like an iceberg
I have already accepted that his
Self-imposed celibacy has nothing to
Do with me anymore

That was what I thought until
One fine day he came up to me
All lovey dovey with me
I understood his advances
My blood was boiling

My eyes were burning and
Staring him down
Angrily I told him off
He went away mad and
That was the start of my nightmare

NO HONEY NO MONEY

She was fast asleep
It was way past midnight
Her nine – year - old son was
Sleeping soundly beside her

Suddenly she felt something
Bright flickering
On her eyes and
Her big toe was being shaken

Half - awake she understood
It was the creep's torchlight
It was his way of saying
B**ty call

She sighed
Quietly she went
To his room
Her heart was in tatters

Emotionally and
Financially blackmailed
She had no choice but
To submit

When she turned
To a family member
For help all she got was
'You chose your man'

Just close your eyes and
Pretend
He is a celebrity
Let him have his way

Tears streaming
Down her face
She did just that
When it was over

Quietly she washed up and
Return to her room and
Sobbed into her pillow
This is no way to live

Sigh! Those incidents were
Twenty plus years ago
Today he can no longer
Touched her
A mild stroke had freaked him out!
Hallelujah!

SIDE NOTE:
Twenty plus years ago that's how
l lived my life with dread and fear
in my heart while keeping a straight face
to my boys and at work

THE MAN IN THE NEXT ROOM

I have a man
Sleeping in the
Next room
He's none other than
Sigh….
I hate to say it
My spouse

In the beginning
He sleeps there
For his personal
Health reasons
Later he is there
For all the
Wrong reasons

If that room
Could speak
It would have told
Many a tale

To make grown men
Mad

I have absolute
No empathy
Only a sense of
Spousal duty
For that man
In the next room
Or as I would prefer
His sleeping quarters

LOVE?
Did someone mention
LOVE?
After what he's
Done to me
Please don't make my toes laugh!!

SIDE NOTE:
As a woman of faith FORGIVENESS
I have dispensed
As a human being
How am I to forget?

MISSING LOVE

LOVE!!!
Where are you?
Where did you go?
I have been waiting
For you since
Infancy
Childhood
Adulthood
Matrimony
Not once did I
Feel your presence
If I did it was
Merely passing by
LOVE!!!
I'm at the
Winter of my life

Perhaps only God
Will love me and not you
You've hurt me enough.

TRAGEDY

Sometimes in
Moments of dark despair
I took a walk down memory lane
To reminisce
How one foolish mistake
Had taken me down a path
Strewn with adversities
Toil and pain
So much so 1 believed
It'd make a good Shakespearean tragedy
Tears just welled up and
Rolled down
Sigh!
When will 1 see
Better days?

STRANGER

You don't
Understand
You don't
Get me
You never will

I'm sensitive
Sensitive
To my emotions
I'm in touch
With my soul

I'm a poetess
Without words
I'm nothing
Like I'm nothing
Without God;

You've made me
To be who I am

Thanks to you
I've inked them all
That I've become

I gave you me
But
You broke me
Broke my spirit
Broke my heart;

I may STILL wear
Your name
But....
In my eyes
A stranger you are

Since the day
You blackmailed me
Emotionally
You've messed me up
Mentally

Oh! Woe is the day
I met you!!!

DEADLOCKED

You and 1
Our affinity
As spouses
Have reached
The end of the
Line

From roommates
To
Housemates
To
Mere tenants
We are deadlocked

I have committed
My life to this matrimony
Put my trust in you because
1 loved you and

l believed in you
Nothing else matters
This matrimony has
Become an
Unholy alliance
You put me down
You neglected me
You walked all over me

You used your excuses to
Justify your actions
I nearly died from all your
Emotional threats and
Marital abuses but
God is great

His Divine Intervention
My salvation -
Your wake - up call
Look at you now
A pale shadow of your
Narcissistic self

This is a hung marriage
I only take care of

Your basic needs
You have never loved me
It's time for me to
Seek my own happiness

BECAUSE OF YOU

You and your
Honey-coated tongue
Sweet and a smooth talker
That you are
You had me fooled and 1 fell
Hook, line and sinker
For you

Because of you
I initiated a 'mutiny'
I fought for you
Believing that you
Are so deserving of my love
Gosh! Because of you
A stupid fool 1 became

Because of you
I felt so ashamed
I lost my dignity
I lost my pride

I lost my self esteem
Most of all
I lost myself

Because of you
Cancer came for me
Due to the tremendous
Duress you put me through
The thought of me dying and
Leaving the boys with you
Made me fought to survive

Because of you
I fell into the abyss but 1
Crawled my way back with
Every breathe 1 had
While you - God had
Dealt with you
You got what you deserved
A mild stroke – compliments from Him

MY AWESOME HEART

It has been a part of me
Since the day I was born
Through the good times and
Mostly the bad plus all
The others in between

It has taken so much beating
Physically – the punishment
From the caning as a child
To the emotional pain
In marrying wrong

I am sorry that you have me
As your mistress dear heart
In my quest for love
In my twilight years
I still made you suffer

You have been excellent
In keeping me alive physically

Emotionally I am such a failure

Such a loser

You don't deserve that

I know you hear me

I feel all the brokenness

I see all the scars

I'll try to heal you

In time you will be alright

For now, let's just

Comfort

One another as best we can

I'll do my best not to hurt you

Again

I DON'T LIVE HERE ANYMORE

Twenty plus years ago
In the year 2003
Something bad happened
In the second half of
That year
It was so tumultuous
That l can still recall
Every bit of that incident

Up to that point in my life
I was a neglected spouse by
A man who suddenly
Decided to choose celibacy
Over me
Time moved on
Into five miserable
Long years

Lo and behold
In June of that year

He decided to end his
Celibacy and came
Looking for his honey
Unfortunately, his honey
Had frozen into an iceberg
In those five long years;

Rejection upon rejection
I had thrown at him
The man 1 knew had become a
Monster as the days
Wore on
I had my boys to protect and
I also had a very
Stressful situation at work;

This iceberg had to thaw
Quick time because he was
Holding the boys as collateral
What can 1 do
Yield to his conjugal demands
Nothing could make me feel
More despicable
Than those hideous acts

Cancer was actually
My saving grace or
So, l thought but sadly
After all my chemo
Treatments - he was waiting
I had barely recovered
I was ready to give up
It's a do or die situation;

It had to take a
Divine Intervention to
Put a stop to everything
Praise the Lord indeed
Took a while to readjust
I have learned to move on
In my mind
I don't live here anymore!

SIDE NOTE: l really wanted this part of
my past to be a closed chapter and
do my very best not to rake it up again!!

BACKSTABBED

l didn't know
The impact of
That word
Till l became a newlywed
Living in the ancestral home

A house full of
Brothers-in-law
With their wives
Thrown in the mix
Life is a drama
Waiting to unfold

Poor naive
Innocent me
Had no inkling
That my words
Were tales
Meant to be spun;

Reality bites
When 1 became
An outcast
Ostracised for
My twisted and
Misconstrued statements;

Five years of
Continuous
Backstabbing
Had metaphorically
Created holes
On my back;

A new abode
I quickly sought
Not a moment too soon
For 1 dread to think of
My premature demise
In that ancestral home!!!

TRAUMA

2003
l didn't ask for this
I didn't ask to be
Afflicted with cancer and
Subsequent PTSD
That tragic year
With the onslaught from
Marital abuse puts
My health under severe
Duress

Eventually
A cancer diagnosis
I was dealt with
I thought it was a
Blessing in disguise
Why? Well, I thought
The abuse
Would stop and

I could pit my
Chances with cancer

It's a do or die situation
The lesser of two evils
Sadly no! I won against
Cancer but the abuse
Continued
Once again
l was hapless but
This time l had
Divine help
A MILD STROKE delivered

Not a moment too late
Not a moment too soon
I was saved but the
Repercussions was waiting
My struggles to
Regain my health and to deal
With PTSD
I still have to care for my boys
It was a long and arduous journey
Thank God I survived

BAFFLED

Sometimes
In my utmost
Lonely moments
I just wish
I have a
Beautiful
Family;

A closely knit
Bonded
One
Full of love
Who does
Everything
Together;

I would begin
To imagine
The fun
The joy

We could have
Not estranged
Like now;

The trips
We'd go on
Like this
Long weekend
Break
Instead of each
To their own;

Is it my fault
Is it my doing
Have l not
Raise
My boys right
With love
So why?

ANGST

You're no longer
My music
You're no longer
My cup of tea
We're no longer
On the same page
You have stripped
Ripped all that is me

Yes!!!
I may have
Chosen you even
Fought to have you
Tragically
In that process
I have also sealed
My own fate
However

God has handed

What you deserved

I am at peace now

TALKING TO WALLS

Walls, walls, walls

Four-sided concrete in my room

Walls, walls, walls

Rebounding my inner echoes of gloom;

Walls, walls, walls

My ultimate substitute for friends

Walls, walls, walls

Having them around – a foregone trend;

Walls, walls, walls

Pictures and portraits on you – I should hang

Walls, walls, walls

Instead, my knuckles on you – I sometimes bang;

Walls, walls, walls

Walls have ears – they say

Walls, walls, walls

Come! Hear me out in all my dismay

Walls, walls, walls

My ultimate companion – till the end of my days!

TRUE LOVE

What does true love
Feels like
Is that feeling the same
During courtship and after?
It should be isn't it
It should be an
Extension of the courtship love

Two people deeply in love
Ready to embark on a
Lifelong journey of
Commitment and starting
A family
I was all so eager and
Ready to start

A new future together but
Life had other ideas
My happy bubble went bust
I was in for a rude awakening

I was hoodwinked
He was a wolf in
Sheep's skin and

I was his prized catch of
A trophy wife
The man 1 knew
Wasn't all he professed
To be and 1 fell for it
Hook, line and sinker
I fell flat on my face

Till this very day
I constantly
Guilt trip myself
I was young and stupid
My goose was cooked
Love? Ha!
Bummer!

When he feels like it
He'll goes lovey dovey
Every time there was an
Ulterior motive

Most times
He took me for a
'LULU' (ignorant fool)

A doormat and there
Is no equality
In these forty plus years
I have been taken for
Granted
Neglected and finally
Abused

I constantly asked and
Brow beat myself
Is this how true love
Supposed to be?
A spouse - a wife
Should be loved
If not adored and respected

For she is your life partner
My ugly past is
Behind me now
I await God's timing

For 1 am sure as hell am
Ready to start over

This time no more
Wearing peaky blinders
I know what 1 DON'T NEED
The man 1 am giving my love to
Will be everything
That CREEP of a spouse isn't!

WHEN ALL IS SAID AND DONE

When 1 looked at you from afar

My mind zoomed back

To the beginning

Courtship

Marriage

Neglect

Abuse

How you have evolved

From a thirty something

To a seventy something

To the man you are now

Time has not been kind

To you - you deserved it

You almost killed me

Not physically but through

Your mind games

My PTSD will come to

Torment me

When l looked you in the eye so

I can't stand

The sight of you anymore

BIRD IN A GILDED CAGE

I am but
A lonely little
Bird
Perched on the
Bar of my
Wide open cage;

Other birds hardly
Dropped by
They would love to
Until they saw
The shackles
On my feet;

If there were any
That came by
It was
To know why my
Cage door is wide
Open

I told them
I could fly anywhere
With the shackles on
Eventually 1 still have
To return to
My gilded cage

The other birds
In unison agreed
You're not one of us
They said
We fly to wherever we
Please;

Whichever tree
We choose to rest
That's our home
Though you live
In a gilded cage
You have no freedom

You may look like
A bird and a
Pretty one at that but
You're restrained

Freedom is our right
For survival;

We're sorry but
We must go now
Don't be sad maybe
You'll be set free
One fine day
See you next time;

I watched as they
Flew off in flocks
Tears welling up
I hung my head
When will 1 ever be free
From this gilded cage??

———————————

ELUSIVE LOVE

I was born
To be
Given away
A taboo child
A third female
In a line of two
There was no
Love for me

My biological parents
Gave me up
At forty days old
My father was gender bias
I became
Someone else's
Only daughter
Among four boys

In an authoritarian
Traditional

Foster family
Life was tough
Especially after
Foster mom died
There was no love
For me either

I have spent
A life time
Searching for love
That l deserved
For l was born next to
Valentine's Day
Love was second
Nature to me

It did come in
Many forms
In a first love
That failed and left
In a rebound love
That was a farce
With ulterior motives
My fate was sealed

I was in for the worst
Emotional rollercoaster
Ride of my life
Leaving me
Abused
Damaged
Broken
Disappointed!!!

It seemed 1 do not
Have any affinity with love
Still 1 persevered because 1
Believed in love
I am love itself and 1 have
Much to give
I will continue to hope until
My dying day!!

AH MA

Ah Ma! Ah Ma!
Here I am talking to you
In Cantonese while looking
At my baby photo
Sitting on your lap
With tears overflowing
I tried to rake
My brain of memories
Spent with you
Not much
Only that of us going
To the movies with Ah Pa

Ah Ma! Ah Ying is
All grown and then some
I know you love me but fate
Took you away
Ah Ma!
Everything changed

The day you left and
I still miss you

SIDE NOTE:
My foster mom died when I
was nine years old. Ah Ying is
my Cantonese Chinese name
I was inadvertently blamed for
her death because they said I
was a child of bad fortune.

LATE BLOOMER

My childhood was
Unhappy
I grew up
An introvert
Speak when spoken to
Kind of upbringing

My puberty
At times
Stoic
At times
A teenage rebel
Unloved

Whatever
Inborn talents
I had was
Never discovered

Never nurtured
Nobody bothered

I was constantly
Deemed useless
A loser
Soggy mud
That won't even hold up
On walls

Now in my twilight years
I have found my niche
In cooking, baking, singing
Painting and writing
I seem to revel in them
They brought me so much joy

Such an awfully late
Bloomer am I
With a tinge of
Regret
I sigh
I wish

Those who
Wrote me off
Are still alive to
See me now
Would they be proud and
Beamed with pride?

A REQUIEM FOR MY SAD SOUL

Lying on my bed
On a hot Saturday afternoon
Reeling over some
Heart wrenching
Emotional issues

My memories set sail
Going back to the day
I was born
Accompanied by the
Songs of the sirens

My father
Looked at me with disgust
Away with her – he said
Perhaps we will have
Beter luck

Better luck he did have
After I was adopted

Six boys came in succession
I had a new set of parents
With four male siblings

Life was good till Ah Ma died
When I was nine
Life changed and
Love left too thus
I spent a life time searching

From hence on
Love became my crusade
To pursue in childhood and
In adulthood

Even in matrimony
True love was never
Really present only a
Tumultuous livelihood
With love that looked like
A mirage
Teasing and taunting me

YOUNG & FEARLESS

I was eighteen
You were twenty-five
I was your student
You - my lecturer
Hence the story began

College
Our very first encounter
Poetry drew us together
That motorbike of yours
Pulled us even closer;

You became
My first love
My virgin kiss was
Yours to own
Talk about explosiveness

It was a difficult
Relationship

Obstacles abound
Hush hush
All the way

Yet
Our love was so true
So pure
Absolutely
Intoxicating;

Sadly
Like most first loves
It was short-lived
Spewed with objections
The Romeo and Juliet kind

Fate
Dealt us a cruel hand
You left for the land of the
Star spangled banner
I stayed behind;

They speak of first loves
As always

Unforgettable
Sigh!
So true;

Till this day
I will never forget
That fire in our love
We were so
Young and fearless!!!

RAINY DAY FLASHBACK

It rained this morning
While l was at the diner
Having breakfast
It was a mere
Flash shower

The rain
Affected my thoughts
It made me sad
Made me remember
The past

To a time when
I was in a relationship
With my first love
We were riding happily
In his motorbike

A flash shower
Rained down

We were quite
Drenched and had
To seek cover

Under a flyover we went
Seeking shelter
Young and fearless
The rain didn't dampen our
Spirits

Ah....those days of
Being in love
Everything was beautiful
All it matters was we had
Each other and our young love

I wish to have
A feel of that
Kind of love again
Innocent, pure and free
I know it's impossible

Back then 1 was nineteen
Today 1 am sixty four

My life's journey was filled

With adversities

Finding a good love - a rarity

UNEASY VIBES

This home became silent
Once again
There is no one home
This shroud of loneliness
As 1 often called it
Is hovering over me
I don't like this feeling
Not even a miniscule bit

It makes me develop
Moody vibes
At this moment
All 1 need are hugs
To have someone
I need someone
I need human contact
I need human connection

I'm trying to get customized
With solitude

I can't! 1 can't! I can't!
I'm hyperventilating
It's driving me nuts
My body is reverberating
With really yucky vibes
Oh! Lord! Why am 1 like this?

I can't! 1 can't! I can't!
I'm hyperventilating
It's driving me nuts
My body is reverberating
With really yucky vibes

CLUELESS

My soul
Provides me
With a distraction
From this
Miserable present
By getting me
To be her scribe
Tunes from her howls

However
There are days
When she is silent
Unable to even howl
Not a beep comes
Out of her
Affecting me to deal
With this despair

That's the time
When the Devil

Starts to mess
With me
Nonsensical
Thoughts
Fly across my
Mind;

l struggle to
Push them away
To counter them with
Positivity
But it's always futile
I find myself
Feeling clueless
Feeling lost

TIME AND LONELINESS

Loneliness
Don't sit well with me
I feel I'm being
Caged in by loneliness
While time continues to move
In its constant pace

I have a schedule
Where l fly out of
My cage to do whatever
I need to do
Ultimately l will need to
Return to my cage

These metaphoric
Shackles
On my ankles control

Me from breaking free
Free from this family
I have no life!

LONELY NIGHTS

Sometimes
The night is long and lonely
It's quiet with the
White noise
For company
Then you feel as if the walls
Are closing in on you

Prior to 2018
Insomnia was
My best friend
I did everything 1 could
Counting sheep
Deep breathing
Nothing worked

Help came in 2018
In the form of a therapist
Who ventured out
To start his own practice

That insomnia
Finally had a name
Dysthymia

I also suffer from PTSD
I'm on medication and finally
I can have
A good night's sleep
With fuzzy dreams but no
Nightmares
Praise God!

It's hard to move on
With PTSD emerging
In my dreams
Sometimes
Anyway, 1 am learning
To cope but
Being alone is rather sad

That's when 1 am so grateful
For those medication
To help get me
Through the night

I don't want to be alone

I can't do 'being alone'

I need love in my life

CONVERSATIONS DEPRIVED

She has cravings
Like that of a
Pregnant woman
She is starving
Like a homeless person
For what? Dang!
For good ole
Conversations

She wasn't born
Yesterday you know
She's nobody fool
She has so much
Knowledge
Accumulated
Over the years and
She is still learning

Pick her mind and
You would be

Gobsmacked
How this Asian lady
Has more western mindset
Than an Asian
Nevertheless, she has never
Forgotten her roots

Tragically
That is exactly the reason
She has no
Like-minded friends
Even those of Chinese educated
Made her feel like
A stick in the mud
Life could never be lonelier

Most times
She talks to God
She knows He hears her
She sings to the walls
They rebound
The song back to her
Like an amplifier
Loud and clear

By sunset
She sighs
She pops her
Medication to call it a day!

HARSH REALITY

Like every young girl
Growing up during puberty
I have my own silly notions of
Prince Charming and
Happily, ever after

As I began to mature into
Womanhood
Life sucker punched me
In the head
Busted my fairy tale dreams

My life is not mine to own
I had discovered
It had already been
Mapped out
According to the elders' wishes

My first love was met
With disapproval

Too poor – they snubbed
He can't even support himself
Let alone me

I was helpless
I was shattered
Today…
He is a renowned
Professor in the academia world

Rebound love
Came along
Once again
A UNANIMOUS NO was
Handed down

Poor family background – they say
This time I retaliated
I've had enough
A mutiny I staged
The elders had to relent

Unbeknownst to me
I set up my own downfall
I married a wolf in sheep's clothing

No use crying over spilled milk
I made my bed I'll sleep in it

Thus
Began the four decades plus of
Unthinkable struggles
Facing all of life's
Threatening storms

My little girl's fairy tale of
An ever after was one big
Foolish lie replaced by a
Harsh reality that this young
Woman never saw coming

SILENCE

I deal with silence
Most hours
Everyday
I'm grateful for Spotify
To break the monotony

When silence persists
The voices
Inside my head
Come hauntingly
Out to play

It's not my
Choice
It's just the
Way my life is
Right from birth

Given a better
Alternative

I'd be engaging
In fruitful
Conversations

No such luck
I carry the
Weight
Of loneliness
For far too long

Sometimes seeking
Distractions
Is of no help
Makes me more
Miserable
I ended up
With my head
Hang low
Feeling so absolutely
DEFEATED!

GHOST IN A SHELL

This house
Is not a home
Tis nothing
But a haunted shell
Devoid of warmth and
Life

The aura of
Human souls - missing
Eerie in its
Silence
Cold like a mortuary
Unapologetic as it is

With me constantly
Wandering through
It's empty hallway

Lonely like a

Ghostly singular

Occupant!!!!

LONELY TABLE JUST FOR ONE

It's a forgone
Conclusion
That l am a loner
I move about
In town - alone;

It is very seldom
To see me walking with
Company
Even groceries l
Handle it alone;

At my usual diner
I'm a regular
Patron and
I'm also very chummy
With the owners;

Has it always been
Like that?

Yup! More years than
I can count
It's part of my life;

When l was much
Younger
It doesn't bother me but
With age feelings change
I miss having company;

Company for chitchat
Company for
Joyful banter
Food tastes much better
Loneliness pushed aside;

If there are no
Changes at all
I'm afraid it
Shall remain
Lonely table just for one

ALONE

Alone, alone
This lonely life beckons
No friends, no buddies
Only me, myself and I;

Alone, alone
This lonely life awakened
One sliced bosom to lament
One dented pride to defend;

Alone, alone
A lonely life to reckon
Chemo cocktail - a must have menu
Chemo hangover - a physique transformed;

My heart - it trembles
My lips - they mumble
To walk not, to travel not
This demented path - ALONE

FALLEN ANGEL

In the still of the night
Amidst the
Cold winds that
Blows and
Slithers through
The trees in the forest
Creating a howling echo

A pack of howling
Wolves gathered
Beneath
The glow of
The full moon that
Weaves in out through the
Silhouette of the trees

There among the echoes
A lonely angel's cry is heard
Her wings are clipped
She is lost with no

Hope to fly home
Home - where love is
Waiting for her!!!

SWAP

Do you know
What it is like
When the
White noises
Seems louder than
The music on
Spotify;

Do you know
What it is like
When you scroll
Through
The contacts
On your
Mobile phone;

Only to realize
There isn't
Really
Anyone you

Could call or
Text for a chat;

They are either
Working
Being
Soccer mom or
Living
On the other side
Of the world - sleeping;

In that
Clear and distinct
Moment
You realize
How absolutely
Terrifying
Lonely - you are;

If you cannot
Comprehend
How 1 feel
Come!

Let's swap

Walk a mile

In my shoes!!!!

TRINET POETRY
(7 LINES POETRY)

REGRETS

My choice

My bad

I was blinded by love

To choose you as my spouse

You took me for granted

You abused me - you did

You creep!!!

SHROUDED IN GLOOM

A hot hot afternoon
At 89.6F/32C
I am into my second
Set of home clothes
There's laundry to be
Put away
A job l do not relish
For valid reasons

When freshly laundered
Clothes needed to
Be put away
Into respective rooms
It is 'his' room that
I dread to walk in
I would be awash with
Queasiness

Even though it won't take
More than five minutes

In an instant my hopeless
Brain starts to rebel
Sending signals to my body
The PTSD then comes
Invading and l'd dashed to
My room to calm down

It doesn't happen
ALL the time
It's especially apparent
When l feel
The loneliness overriding
My quiet surroundings
A situation l have no
Control over

Ultimately
Depression comes on
As l try to get a grip of
My mind
Shrouded in gloom
Sets my brain tethering
Between sobriety and
Melt down

Twenty plus long years
That is how long
This home of mine
(in my name) and
That room with memories of
Those despicable acts
Continues to be a
Thorn at my side!!!

CRAZY

I'm hopelessly down

Unwell and unsound

My mind

Is in shambles

I carry a frown

I speak to myself

Way much too loud

Enough to be heard

In the midst of a crowd;

Am I crazy

Or just

Plain blue

Be kind to tell me

I'm without a clue

So lonely, so lonely

I'm going adrift

I need someone,

If not God

To give me a lift;

I hear and I fear

The voices within

This static

This madness

It's stretching me thin;

They prod me to tears

They drive me insane

I just might hack it

With a final refrain!

LONELINESS MAGNIFIED

Today's gloomy weather
Feels like autumn
It's not! It did not have that
Autumn chill
It's a Saturday night
With no one at home
Even in the comfort of
My room
This loneliness is MAGNIFIED

I miss being hugged
I miss sharing loving
Conversations
I miss being loved
Tonight, my bed
Looms larger and colder
All those messy thoughts threaten
To surface and thank God
The meds took care of that

LONELY EXISTENCE

Look at her
Love that smile
So, bedazzling
So, captivating
What did you say?
Depressed?
Rubbish!!

I have never
Seen a more
Sublime and
Blissful smile
On a woman
Depressed?
Don't make my toes laugh

Yes! My dear virtual
Friends
That is how
I learn to cope

My smile
Is sincere and warm

It shows the joy of
Being out
To be seen albeit
Alone
I project
A warm persona even
If I am chatting with the waiters

I lead a very lonely
Existence
I posed the question
To my therapist
He replied – 'they are not
In your league'
Perhaps so…

Writing poems
In English
Have made me lean
Towards a Caucasian
Mindset
Still! I have not forgotten my roots

I can still converse
In a smattering of
Local dialects and
Our National Language
Cantonese/Mandarin
Hakka and Hokkien
It is no big deal here

In summation
I concur
My smile is mesmerizing
I am no fake
This smiling skill
Had been honed since
A young age

After every caning session
I was forced to smile
Later I realized to quickly
Smile first
That helped me to escape
The caning several times
Sick right?

I suppose as time goes by
I am resigned to this

Predicament
No man would want a
Woman with
Unresolved issues
It's morally wrong!!!

SIDE NOTE:
Divorce is not an option
and so that is why I am
unattainable

____

HURT

It's an act....
Done to me
More times than
I can remember
In this life time
It led me to think
That it is my fate

As a child
Hurt....
Comes from
Caning....
To make me
Toe the line
Lest 1 misbehaved

Physical hurt
Is nothing
Compared to
Words

Directed at myself
Feelings
Unfiltered

Even then
I was relatively
Able to appease
My feelings
With my head held high
With a smile to go
To move on

However
Hurtful words
That came from
Family members
Is like a direct stab
To the heart
You bleed unseen

It is my
Achilles Heel
The emotional
Wound

Stays gaping for
A long long time
A perpetual open wound

It is also
The kind of hurt
That affects my soul
So difficult to
Appease
For it is where she
Howls the loudest

MY SO - CALLED LOVE STORY

I had only been in love
Twice - as in real time
Face to face
The old school way
Prim and proper

He was my first love
We met in college and
We clicked over
English Literature
How appropriate

We were both romantics
To the core
He had dreams on a
Scholarship to the USA
He wanted me to go along

Unfortunately
Our relationship

Did not receive my
Family's blessing
We were forced to breakup

I had to play the bad guy
Not wanting him to pine
The scholarship was important
I broke up with him
He was so torn

I had to be cruel in order
To be kind
After he left 1 cried buckets
My foster family couldn't care less
It was my first taste of a heart break

I told myself that
The next man 1 meet
A man who professed
Sincere love and concern
I'll make sure I'll fight for him

The man in the next room
Was that second love or

Shall 1 say
Love on the rebound
He was so slick in wooing me

No blessing from family too
This time 1 stood my ground
Family relented and 1 went
Out of the frying pan and into the fire
The rest was my miserable history

IDLE MIND

I am an introvert
Little by little
I'm beginning
To feel
Closeted more and more;

When one has lived
A lonely existence
For such a long time
That scenario soon
Becomes me;

Being at home
Those long hours
Is a perfect time for
The Devil to mess
With my mind;

You know what
They say

About the idle mind
Being the Devil's
Workshop;

Oh yes! He had tried
Many many times
Serving up negative
Thoughts in my mind
Trying to pull me down;

Some days l will block out
Those thoughts by
Singing
Some days writing poems
Or pray him back to Hell;

I really can't afford
For him to
Mess with me
My years are waning
Let me live it well!

PUSHING BUTTONS

Patience
Is a virtue
I'm often told and
Patience
Is portrayed
Best
In my works of art;

In relationships
My good natured
Patience
Is often tested
To its
Saturation point
Time and time again

So! Do not
Continue to
Push my button of

Patience

You won't like me

It isn't very becoming

For l will become a volcano!!!

A POET'S PRAYER

May I always
Be led by the
Emotions from my soul
To ink what I feel
Till the quill runs dry

May I pray that
Those likeminded
Ones like me
Finds inspiration
To ink what they feel

We poets do
What we do best
We ink our thoughts
What we cannot
Express verbally;

Through our words
You'll know us

Understand us
Quicker than
Quick Draw Mcgraw;

We poets
Love our words
Our poetical ammunition
Our buddies in
Good times and bad;

To know us
To understand us
Read our works
We're in a special
League of our own!!!

This is my ardent prayer
To all who appreciate poetry

LOVE'S RICH BOUNTY

You will see my love
For what it is
Full of gratitude
To the man who
Accepts my past and present

Pure because
l am holding out
For the right man
Therefore, it is not tainted
Like a lotus it awaits to bloom

I have been short changed
I have been denied true love
All that l had before
Came with an agenda
Unbeknownst to me

My love is bountiful
There is still room

For a rich harvest
Only if 1 am loved well
In the hands of the right man

TAKING BACK MY LIFE

I shall not be taken for a ride

Be ignored and mistaken

For a fool

I shall not be put down

Be made to feel like a clown

I shall not be mistreated

My feelings used and cheated

I shall be beautiful

I shall be mindful

Living life being humble and cheerful

I shall love myself

With absolute candour

I execute no strategies

I offer no apologies

To the Valley of Death – I have been

I've returned

I've survived

I'm not done with life
What don't kill ya
Only made you stronger

I now stand tall
I now stand strong
No more happiness denied
All my emotional chains
Broken

Never ever bind me again
For my peace and dignity
I no longer suffer fools
I shall put up a fight
So, stay out of my sight!!

LACED WITH BLOOD

Ever since 1 have picked up
The pen to start my
Poetical journey
I have realised one cold
Hard fact;

It was God who
Led me to that
Opportune moment
Where 1 found an
Online poetry platform;

Yippee!
I have enough
Poetical bullets
For this newbie to
Enter the poetry scene;

However, 1 was also
Ignorant to

The rules and
Regulations as l
Kept firing away;

That landed me in
'Poetical jail' on
A few occasions
A real lesson on
Poetical etiquette

Now l have learned to
Pace myself in
Inking my poems
To allow the pain inside
To slowly find release;

Each poetical bullet
Have a story to tell and
They are laced with blood
All about my past
From childhood till now;

There are very very few
Genuine
Happy memories

That l can
Call upon to write;

I am still a
Shackled bird
Living in bondage
I feel no love
From my sons too;

Married men who
Hardly
Dropped by or call
Instead, I am at their
Beck and call

The day my poetry facade
Changes
Is when l am free from all
Encumbrances
A truly liberated woman!!!

MY POETIC INK

My life is
A story told
In the lines and
Stanzas
Of my poetry

My tears
My pain
My grievances
Are inked down
For all to read

If through my poetry
There is a sense of
Relativity and A-ha moments
Then read on to understand
How 1 survived

I hardly
Write about joy

Happiness
They are rather
Rare

The rawness
The honesty
My vulnerabilities
Are laid bare
No holds barred

To hold back means
I have nothing to write
I might as well
Break the quill
Pour away the ink!!

MY OWN WOMAN

I'm no man's
Possession
I'm no man's
Object of desire
I'm no bimbo too
I'm more if not on par
With any man;

I shall not
Be dictated to
No man shall
Back me into a corner
We can negotiate
For 1 am open to
Suggestions;

I may seem
Vulnerable
But I am strong
When necessary

I can hold
My own
Against any man;

From where 1 was
To where 1 am now
My body
Abused
My spirit
Battered
My soul - broken;

I have survived
Everything that
Life hurled at me
No more cowering
Never again
Don't believe?
Just watch!!!

EYES

My eyes
Are the window
To my soul
My face is like
An open book
A vast array of moods

Everything
From happiness or sadness
Are written on my face
Visible through my eyes
Unless I chose
Not to otherwise

My soul is constantly
Disturbed
My soul is always
Howling
My soul feels
Unhappy and lost

Until I can figure out

My issues

A feeling of morose

Hangs vagrantly

Around

It is difficult to keep it in

FRAGILE MIND – PTSD

She knows
She had promised herself
To no longer
Dwell on the past
It's history now

Let them be buried
In her heart and
Not even brought
The matter to light
It's just pointless

However
She is still alive
She is still breathing
As long as there is life
She can never forget

She is only human
She is not infallible

She has her fragile
Moments
That can be easily triggered

In her loneliest
Hours
She hear the walls
Speak
They whisper

They whisper to her
What transpires
Within that room
Oh! So long ago
She starts to hyperventilate

She wants to
Scream
Bang the walls
With her fists
Tell them to stop

Stop!!
Reminding her

She wants to
Be strong but
She can't

Ultimately, she ended up
Being a part of
Those whispers
Lost and immersed
In those dreaded memories

____

LIVE LAUGH LOVE

Those are my three key
Ingredients to a life
Full of contentment and
A partner who shares the
Same ideals

Two heads are
Better than one
With each of us
Working harmoniously
Towards that goal

Throughout
My entire lifetime
I have shed
Enough tears
To fill up a river

Slept on beds of
Cactus

To know what pain is
Enough!
I've had enough!

I fervently pray for someone
To rescue me from
This hell I'm living in
I have been praying
For so long

Praying feverishly
That sometimes only a
Sigh escapes me but
God knows and each time
I hear a 'IN MY TIME'

THE LITTLE GIRL IN ME

There resides in me a goofy
Litle girl who would
Love to come out
To play when she
Senses that I am having
A good time

She wants
To join in the fun too
Oh! She is the life of
The party
There would be
So much joy and laughter

I enjoy her company too
I would be in my element
Coming up with
Spontaneous silly jokes
I adored that little girl

Over the years
She seldom gets
To come out to play
I have never had the chance
To laugh like that
Pranking cheekily

I missed those
Magical moments
Instead of having
To be reduced to
A heap of miserable
Emotional mess

HYPHEN

Between my birth and
My death
There is a long hyphen
In between them in which
Lies the story of
My life

How have I lived my life?
Are there many
Important milestones
To be proud of?
Have I lived a life
Worthy of praise
I'm sorry
I have failed

Inside that hyphen
Lies a thousand

Painful tales
Love and happiness
Never existed in
That hyphen

A WOMAN WITH NO LIFE

Forty plus years of a
Tumultuous marriage
I have finally reached
A peaceful plateau

Yes! There were moments
When my life was
In danger but
The thought of my boys
Losing me

Gave me a reason and the
Will to survive
Through cancer and
Abuse
I faced them all

So, now
I have a new role
In life – a survivor and a

Woman with no life
A lonely introvert

Thank God for small
Pleasures as in
My art and vocal classes
I never take my life
For granted

My poetry is my
Craft and instrument
For my inner voice
My soul
To release my pain

My predicament
In this marriage
I am leaving it to fate
I'm seen but not heard
An empty nester

As long as the abuser
Is still alive
I am in

No moral position
To start a new relationship

As they say
You win some
You lose some
This society has little pity
For a woman like me

ENIGMA

My persona is
Multi-faceted
Like an onion
As you peel away
The layers
My story is a tale
Waiting to be told

In every station of my life
Childhood
Adulthood
Motherhood
One can find many
Episodes of
A serial drama

I am an enigma
A mystery
A woman

Worth knowing

Worth understanding

Worth empathizing

Finally worth loving

POETICAL LANDSCAPE

One fine day
When I am led
Out of this
Toxic environment
When I am able
To rebuild my life
With whatever time
I have left

My writings
In particular
My poetical landscape
Will see a change
In the tone
In the façade
In its theme

No more
Dark morbid
Writings or

Bitter rantings
When love
Becomes my heart's
Core center
Everything changes

Stay with me
Bear with me
You! Who have known
Where I came from
When that day
Arrives
I ask nothing but
Your prayers and blessings

I have faith in my God
I believe that one day
Will come
I will continue to pray
Unceasingly
As long as there is still
Life in me

THE JOURNEY TOWARDS HEALING

After forty plus
Years in a
Tumultuous marriage
It is safe to say that
My poor heart has had
Enough

The emotional beatings
That it took on my behalf
Is truly
Admirable but
The scars it left behind
Are still very sensitive

I need to heal her
I know that but I don't
Have the solution
To my predicament

I am still living in a
Toxic environment

The man in the next room
Has deteriorating
Cognitive issues and hard
At hearing
A perfect excuse for him to
Be held NOT ACCOUNTABLE

What can I do now?
Absolutely nothing
That creep and I are
Engaged
In a longevity war
May the healthiest one wins

THE THIRST FOR LOVE

There are days
When I am alone
In my room
I'll sit hugging
My knees in a
Corner of the bed

I'll bury my face on
My knees and
Slowly but surely
The tears start to
Trickle down my face
From a whimper to a bawl

It's no secret that this
Loneliness gets to me
I have to have an outlet
Otherwise, I will surely go

Insane

So, help me God

These are the moments

I let my guard down and

Unhinged myself from

The armor of courage

I come undone and

Bare my soul

I longed for love

Love is so sacred to me

An emotion I thirst for but

Many take for granted

Not I, for I have never

Felt loved only used

I'm past my prime now

Gravity is unkind to a

Woman

Rubbing salt to the wound

My predicament prohibits

Me to have any relationship

Therefore, each day
I live a little and I die
A little and soon
The broken pieces of me become
Like HUMPTY DUMPTY

ON A CLEAN SLATE

I am so thankful
God is good to me
I am here on this
Peaceful plateau
No more drama

Under the same roof
In separate quarters
Our lives
To each our own
No questions asked

I will rise
From the ashes of
My own pain
Maritally I'm still
Legally bound

Never mind
Freedom will come

Someday I am sure
On a clean slate
I will chart my own life

I will create my own
Happiness
On my own terms
On my own conditions
My life – my choice

A NEW HOME

A NEW START

This is not a home
A home has voices
A home has sounds of
Chitter chatter with
Occasionally sounds of
Joy and laughter

Instead, this abode
Is deathly quiet and
Mortuary cold
The occupants are
Supposed to be a family but
They live like tenants

There's no joy
To be found here
I want to leave
I need to leave
In order to survive
A totally different environment

So different from the one
That I am in now
Away from him and all
The toxins that he carries
That pollutes
My peace of mind

———————————

SAD AND FORLORN

What is this?
What is this so-called
LIFE – My life?
That day by day
It slowly chips away
A bit of my soul
I hear her mournful
Cries
Asking for
Release
I am still trying to hang on

———————————————

SECOND CHANCES

I have been praying
For a second chance
To allow me to love and
Be loved
For this time, I'm
No longer wearing
Peaky blinders

I hate being physically old
I'm not wired to be that way
I love life but sadly
I rewrote my own fate and
I feel gutted

I have no great expectations
A Godly man he must be
Showering me with
Love and devotion
A relationship with
Built in connectivity

I know! I know!
I am not in the right
Disposition to have it
On paper I'm as good as
A ghost in the wind
Nevertheless
I shall keep on praying and
Waiting

God works in
Mysterious ways
Where there is no way
He will make a way
All things will happen
In MY time not yours
HE said!!!

BE CALM

Look at her
Sitting quietly
Engrossed in deep thought
Even though
It is the dreaded
Month of September

However
She has had
Enough of
All those dark
Memories
That loves to stir up her pain

This year
She is doing her utmost
To keep those memories
At bay
She prays for nothing
But good days ahead

It has been said that
There is no time line on
Healing
When you are still living
In that toxic place

Hence
She will meditate
More regularly
To recalibrate her
Thought process
Peace of mind remains
Her top priority

MY LOVE STORY

It's been years now
Praying, wishing and hoping
Day in day out
Days into weeks
Into months into years

What am I talking about?
Why a chance to write
My own love story of course
The only issue is l have yet
To meet the love of my life

I suppose as long as
I'm still alive l have hope
They say he's just around
The corner but l have bumped
Into more RATS than THE ONE

Seriously! I hope to meet him
While l am still able bodied and

Them wrinkles have yet to
Surface
At my age injuries are a no no

Oh! mama mia
How 1 love to write
My own happy ending
The older 1 get
The slimmer my chances

Mind you! 1 am not going to
Settle this time for any
TOM/DICK/HARRY
I shall proceed with caution
Looking out for red flags

BLESSED

Once upon a time
There lives this
Woman
A victim of a
Tumultuous marriage;

She was young and stupid
Naive and gullible
Who thought she had
Found her knight
In shining armour;

Fast forward
Forty plus years on
This young woman
A twilight woman now
Older and wiser;

Life's bitter lessons
Learned
From every adversity
Filled with
Heartache and pain;

She is stronger
More resilient and
Courageous
Having her mettle
Tested to the limits;

She shines forth
Like gold
Her laughter - infectious
Her smile matches
The brilliance of the sun;

She is a picture
Of confidence
Nothing can ever
Bring her down or
Put her in a corner

She's been there
Done that!!!

SELF LOVE

When the ones
I love
Especially my
Flesh and blood
Are nonchalant
About my
Wellbeing
I won't fret

I'll just sigh
I'll just make a
Mental note
I'll remind myself
That love in
Any other forms
Are also not
Available to me

Once my heart
Understood
I'll learn to find ways
To love myself
Better
I will not depend
On others for
My happiness

Only then
Can l move on
To find
Joy and happiness
In doing the things
I love and
Within myself
My soul would surely thank me

Life can
Wear us down
Hurt us but don't
Ever let it
We must always

Guard our hearts

Be our own

HEALER!!!

MOVING ON

I don't
Look back at
My past
In bitterness
In anger;

All that had
Happened
Were meant
To test my
Mettle;

I did not
Succumb
I survived....
I look back
Only in
Amazement;

I left my past
Where they
Belong
My follies
My lessons
Learned;

I move forward
In clockwork
Manner
With no
Expectations;

HAPPINESS
Is secondary
Have or have not
Irrelevant
All l need is
PEACE OF MIND!

LIVE EACH DAY LIKE YOUR LAST

Wake up
Smile....
Be thankful
Another day
Unfolds before
You;

Spend a few minutes
Ascertaining all necessary
Written instructions
Are where they should be
In folders and within
Eyesight;

Greet your neighbours
If they ever
Cross your paths
One never knows
If that is the last
We see of them;

Be gracious
Have a kind word
Or a smile
For those you
Meet throughout
The day;

Do the same....
For virtual friends
As well....
Cherish the friendship
To be friends online
Is true affinity;

Live blessedly
Die not......
Regretfully!!!!

____

DESERVING BETTER

I deserve better
Better respect
Better loving
Better treatment
As a spouse after
All that had happened
When 1 married wrong

I have been
Hurt
Neglected
Abused
Threatened
For all that
I don't deserve;

I want to
To reclaim
My life
To be free from

From him completely
That despicable spouse but
It's easier said than done;

My life may be at a
Peaceful plateau and
I have every reason
To be grateful but
I have no reason
To be happy
Time is running out;

My life right now
Constantly under
His toxic aura
Every decision
Every action taken will
Have an equal or opposite
Reaction

SOME DAYS

Some days are good
Peaceful and fine
Whiling my time
At the cafe
Inking my poems
On my lap top
At an inspirational pace

Some days are
Cumbersome
Loads of groceries
To carry alone
All the way up to
The third floor of
My apartment

Some days are
In between
Peaceful and quiet
Spent at home

Lazing around or
Sometimes with
Chores to do

Some days are awful
The mood swings
Comes around
Messing with my thoughts
Interrupting my flow
For writing
A writer's block at every level

Whatever days
They turn out to be
I know they'll get better
Don't have
Too many expectations
I don't react now to every
Unpleasant issue

In the affairs of the heart
There is a time for everything
The right one will turn up
To come looking for me

No need to search
I confess a sense of
Urgency in me

Waiting on God's timing
He is never too early
Or too late and
No matter how slim
My chances are
I shall remain nonchalant
My heart will know!!!

THEIR LOVE

Two kindred souls
Who has no idea
That their relationship
Would transcends
Distance and time
To elevate into a beautiful
Bond of being soul mates
Where, love and passion
Collides

LEARNING TO BE ALONE

8.30 PM
The sun had set
A long while ago
This home is
Silent
Empty

Usually
This is the hour
Where loneliness rear
Its ugly head
I get affected and
My mood changes

I must say
I am beginning
To feel better now
I am learning to adjust and
To be comfortable
With myself

Once I can overcome

The neediness of

Wanting to be loved

Sooner or later

I will be happy with myself and

In my own skin

—————————————

TWILIGHT LOVE

Finding love in the
Winter of our lives
In the twilight of our years
Is something so
Amazing and incredible
For we have
Seen and experience
The good, the bad and
The ugly
Nothing surprises us
Anymore
If true love comes along
For me then
It is nothing
Short of a miracle

NIGHT TIME BLUES

My eyes are getting drowsy

Thoughts of you are swirling

Across my mind

Opposite ends of the world

We are at

Tis time to arise

To start your day

I am so filled with love for you

Only you can fill this void

In my heart

You are my soul mate

Our connection runs deep

Let's keep it that way huh?

THE WAY YOU LOVE ME

Spontaneous back hugs
Catching me off guard
Yet it felt so sweet and
The way you nuzzle down
My neck with sensual kisses
You really know what you're doing
I love you with all I have too
Our bodies may be aged but
Our hearts burn with passion

MY POETIC WORLD

I'm often seen but
Not heard
You'd think
This old school of thought
Only apply to kids

In this home
My opinions
Don't really matter
Except for
Household issues

My well being
Is cast aside
Is ignored
Unless
I really LOOK sick

It's fine
In the virtual

World of poetry
I'm seen and heard
I'm respected
I'm LOVED

My thoughts matter
My emotions
Resonate
With all who
Read
My poems

I no longer bemoan
My value
In the eyes of the
Unappreciative
Occupants of
This home

The poetic world
Is my new family

MY POETRY

Appreciate me
As a POET first
Delve into my
Poems and
The messages
They convey

When I post
My poems
With my selfie
It is because

Every one of them
Every expression
Is in corelation
With the theme
I am writing

To further enhance
The subject matter and

To create the
Dynamics in them

Do not assume
I am an object of
Your fantasy
To be oogled at

A true aesthete of
Poetry
Would immerse
Oneself into

The poetic craft
Before looking
Into the picture
As a whole

That is
The true
Appreciation of poetry

MY LIFE IN POETRY

Each of us alive
Is living a life
Full of stories
With past memories

Some of us
Have bad
Memories
Which they wish
Not to talk about

While some
Who have
Happy ones
Chose to constantly
Brag about them

As for me
My life

Is one heck of a
Korean drama
A soap opera

A forty plus episode
Still counting
All of which
I chose to be
The screen writer

Every episode
Full of plots
Twists and turns
Are written in
Poetical form

It is a way
For me to
Purge
Unleash
All of my bitterness

The final episode
Will be written with my

Passing

As an eulogy

MINDFUL LIVING

Go to bed
With a thankful smile
Wake up
With a grateful heart

Thankful for the peace
To have a sweet slumber
Grateful for the chance
To see another new day

Make the day great
Stay active
Be productive
Always go about
With a cheerful heart and
A flashy smile

For negativity
Will not intrude

If positivity stands

Guard

At the door of

One's heart

LOVE ON FIRE

Come here my love

Come sit by my side

Open your arms to

Wrap them around me

Let me gaze at your

Intense steely eyes

Filled with fiery

Passion

Let me feel the heat

When we lock lips

Tender at first

Till it builds into a

Crescendo of desire

Help me to remember

What it is like

To be loved

It's been so long

Twenty plus years is

A long long time

EMOTIONAL SUPPORT

Sometimes
I feel lonely
Sometimes
Needy
I am not cuckoo
Just human

When my
Mouth and my
Heart
Are not in
Cohesiveness
I become a bundle of
Contradictions

I know
Who I am
I also know
Where I am
At this point

In my
Life

What right
Do I have
To accept love or
To love
Another
In return

At best
I can be there supporting
Emotionally and
Vice versa
That is as good
As it gets

Unless
Divine Intervention
Happens
I will be exactly
Where I am
Trapped
Unattainable

MY SCARRED HEART

If you could
Look inside
My heart
You would see
The many many scars

Scars
From a heart
That had been
Wounded
Bled
Healed
With deep
Scars

Some parts
You will find
Overlapping

Scars
That came
From wounds
Barely healed
Only to be hurt
Again

My poor poor
Heart is still beating
Despite
Being disfigured
By those scars

She knows
Life is still
Deathly
Futile
To make a
Change

Somehow
Somewhere
My heavily
Scarred heart

Still finds a reason

To keep on

Beating

MY LIFE

Like a game of chess
One wrong move
One wrong decision and
You've got to find ways
To come back from
The brink of defeat

The stakes are high
Losing is not an option
Every wrong move
You make
Will propel into a
Domino effect

No way to stop
You can't
No matter how hard you try
It's going to run
Its course and then
CHECKMATE

That's my life

Akin to a game of chess

A weakling am I at this game

My opponent outwitted me

I lost the game

My dignity and pride too

My chess queen (me)

Has lost to the King (that creep)

When I think of my fate in reality

How do I make another move

When I am all done in?

BEAUTY IN THE DAY

Look at the day
With positive eyes
You will see
Wonders galore
Full of colours

The soothing
Warmth of
The sun
After a night's
Cold rain

Even the flowers
Bloom gloriously
Basking in the sun
Their colours
Fresh and radiant

There is an aura of
Recharged energy

In a brand – new day
Like a new art canvas
Ready for us to paint the day

With positive eyes
Everything is beautiful

LOVE SPEAKS IN SILENCE

On this
Sandy shore
In the glow of
The evening sunset
We sat – huddled
Together
Caressed by the warm winds

Suddenly you pulled me
Closer
The nearness of
You – thrills me
As we
Watched the tide
Ebbs and flow

You turned to me
Tipped a finger under
My chin to lift my face
To face you

I tensed up as
Your face got closer to mine

Soon we were
Locking lips
At first gently as
Your lips brushed
Against mine and
As our passion intensifies
Our kiss burned like the setting sun

Not a word transpired
Between us only
The look on our eyes
Our heavy breathing
The intimacy of two
Souls in love for
Actions speak louder than words

WHEN LOVE COLLIDE

You and 1

Two oceans

Apart

Like night and day

I dream of us

So very often

What are the

Chances

We will meet?

If Providence

Favours us

It will be like a meteor

Crashing down

All those pent up

Feelings

Emotion unspoken

Unexpressed

Will have us

Colliding into

Each other's arms

The moment

We meet

Oh! Love

Will that day

Ever come?

IN YOUR LOVING ARMS

Hold me in your

Sweet embrace

Envelope me with

The strength of your love

Rock me gently

Let me gaze into your eyes

That speaks of nothing but

Passion

I know you love

My lips in which you find

So desirable

Kiss me and let our love be

Ignited

I LOVE YOU!

RECKLESS LOVE

You've got your eyes on me

Way before you said 'Hello'

I saw you too

Way across the table

You were alone and so was 1

Something clicked

Something very beautiful

The vibes criss crossing

Between us

We held each other's gaze

Yea! Let's get out of here

Let's get reckless with love

SMILING ANTIDOTE

It is way past
My bedtime
My medication
Has yet to kick in
I lie on my bed
Staring at the ceiling

My thoughts start
To roam
I realized there
Isn't one single
Happy moment
Post marriage

Every smile
I offered up
Was my own
Doing

Trying to look
Beyond the hurt

So here I am
Looking past
Beyond
The worst times
Of my life
I'm still smiling

It's what I do
To make life
A tad more
Bearable
Finding reasons
To smile

It gives me
Hope
It helps me
To cope
Through the
Bleakest moments

That is the
Only way
I know how
To survive and
Keep surviving
Till happiness drops by!!!

———————————

INTROVERTED ME

Sociable
Thinker
Anxious
Inhibited
Four main types
I am a little bit
Of all;

Those
Characteristics
Weighs heavily
One over the other
Depending on the
Settings;

I prefer a
Calm quiet
Environment
In order to hear
Myself think

A crowded
Bustling cafe
Will have me
Leaving
In no time;

Loneliness
Has
My imagination
My inspiration
My thoughts
Thriving
Like a well-oiled
Machine;

My lonely life
Not by choice
Has become
My comfort zone
I find myself
Hyperventilating
In a crowd
My emotional

Energy
Drained;

I may come
Across as
Aloof
Antisocial
Among people
But truth is
I'm merely
Observing
I take time to
Warm up;

Whether you
Like me or not
It's not my
Business....
It's your call;

I'm already
Half a century
Plus fourteen
I am who I am

Time is too
Fleeting
To worry about
Petty stuff!!!

HIDING PLACE

There is
A place in the
Deep recesses of
My heart
Where only my soul
Knows

A place
Where l hide
All the cherished
Memories of you
Our time together
With the love we share

The many
Poems
From you to me and
Vice versa
Lines upon lines of
Beautiful ink;

When reality gets
Too unbearable
My soul goes there
To seek refuge
In your words of
Undying love!!!

She will be soothed
She will stop howling
Which in turn
Will make me feel
Happy to know
I'm being loved

AGAINST THE RAGING WAVES

My entire
Forty - two plus years of
A wedded life
Is akin to me
Standing in front of
The raging waves

Tumultuous and
Roaring
Standing firm
To face the adversities
That life had
Dished out to me

After years of
Holding my ground
That raging sea
Had begun to ebb

I'm now in
Peaceful waters

Peaceful waters no doubt
Yet I'm far from happy
I'm doing my best
To live out each day
Until the day when
Freedom is within my grasp

With God who is for me
What can be against me!!?

SET FREE

Come one day
When l am totally
A free woman
My soul will no longer
Haunt me
Taunt me
With her howling
For my poetic facade
Will take on a new
Lease of life and
Happiness can
Come to
Reside for good and if by then
I've found love
It'll be double happiness

I AM STILL A WOMAN

Look at me
Smiling bedazzlingly
Despite being stuck in a
Dead marriage
I'm so over it
Stuck as I am
I make the best of this
Deplorable situation

Look at me
Looking at you
Amusingly
As I articulate in my
Conversations
If I don't let on
Can you tell that
I am missing two body parts?

A mastectomy and a
Hysterectomy

In between seven years
Had reduced me
To a much lesser
Woman physically but
I had no time to mope
I had a lot of surviving to do

I don't miss
One of my 'girls'
She ain't nothing much
To look at in the first place
Neither do I miss my
Temporary housing
For babies as
I am done with childbearing

Losing them
Does not make me
Any lesser of a woman
There are women that I
Know of who are unwilling to
Part ways with their 'girls'
Even if they had a choice of
Reconstruction

Heck! Back in my days
Reconstructive surgery was
Relatively new
I had more important
Matters to consider
My survival against cancer
If I lose my battle what's to
Become of my boys?

Into the unknown
I wage my life
With cancer and there are
Moments that I thought
I couldn't summon
Any more strength but
God is great
He was my pillar of strength

Twenty - two years on
I stand tall with my head
Held high unbothered
I live my life on my own terms
I've found peace because
Divine Intervention had been

Handed down

I am still every bit of a woman

Who deserves to be loved
